I0461722

Where There Is No Vision The People Perish ...

-Proverbs 29:18

-ACKNOWLEDGMENTS-

To every thing there is a season, and a time to every
purpose under the heaven.
—Ecclesiastes 3:1-8, KJV

I thank God for bestowing His purpose and blessing on my life. I now know the darkness of the wilderness was never meant to break me; it was designed to help me break into myself. To my mother, Georgia A. Booth-Price, it is an honor to be your son. My beginnings were forged in darkness and crowned with glory. Just as God spoke at the heralding of existence, and it was so, you gave life to me in this world by calling me your son.

My gratitude extends far beyond the names listed within the margins of these pages and book. It is an impossible task to name everyone who had a hand in shaping the person that I am. Please know that I have thought of you as I wrote this book and have sent you many thanks along the way.

To my siblings: Wesley Booth, Quianna Ellis, Charlotte Cole, and Domonique Crumpton. Thank you for your undying support and encouragement; I believe in myself because you believed in me first.

To my children, Nia Booth, Imani Booth, Niama Booth, and Demetrius Booth Jr., I hope this book serves as a testament to what you are capable of in this world and that I have set an example of how to live that you are proud of.

To my wife, Marilyn Booth, thank you for recognizing the better person who was always deep inside of me. Your love in this life is the foundation I stand upon, making it all worth it. If I could go back in time … I would do it all over again.

-FOREWORD-

If you keep silent at this time, liberation and rescue
will arise from another place ... And who knows
whether you have not attained royalty for such a time
as this?
—Esther 4:14, NASB

Everything in creation follows a divine
order—a rhythm written by the hand of God at the
founding of the world. Simultaneously, as He moved
upon the face of the deep and spoke light into
existence, order was instituted. From the soil beneath
our feet to the fruit that hangs from the branches,
every stage of growth is a sacred reflection of the
human journey. The earth itself testifies to the
process within us—that which is hidden must first be
formed before it can be revealed.

We begin as **soil**—the place where God's
hands first touched creation. It was from the dust of
the ground that humanity was shaped, and we
returned into dust. And yet even dust becomes divine
when it receives the breath of life. In this book, **soil**
represents the condition of the heart—what it

welcomes, what it resists, and what it sustains. In good soil, the Word takes root; in neglected soil, it remains only a shadow of the potential that could exist in the form of a seed.

The **seed** is the mystery of beginnings—small, ordinary, and easily overlooked. Yet within it lies everything it will ever become. The seed does not strive to be a tree; it simply surrenders to the process written within it. Christ spoke often of the seed, reminding us that unless a seed falls to the ground and dies, it remains alone—but if it dies, it produces much fruit (John 12:24, NASB). The seed teaches us obedience to process, trust in hiddenness, and faith in the unseen.

Roots follow. They reach downward before anything rises upward. The unseen always precedes the visible. Roots symbolize depth, strength, and striving—the quiet work of faith, character, and connection. They seek out the unseen rivers of grace and truth that nourish endurance. Roots are our unseen devotion, our discipline, and our dependence on the Source.

And then comes the **fruitfulness**—not as an instant outcome, but as growth evidence of faithfulness through seasons. Fruit is the visible testimony of unseen work. It is what others see and experience when they encounter our lives. *"You will know them by their fruits,"* said Jesus (Matthew 7:16, NASB). Fruit is the outward manifestation of inward transformation. It is the reward of those who tend their soil, protect their seed, and deepen their roots through every storm.

Each element—soil, seed, roots, and fruit—is inseparable from the others. Together they form a divine ecosystem of growth evidence that mirrors the kingdom of God and the condition of the human soul. In this way, we are living trees planted by His design, destined to bear fruit that reflects His glory.

-CONTENTS-

-INTRODUCTION-

For I know the thoughts that I think toward you,
saith the LORD, thoughts of peace, and not of evil,
to give you an expected end …
—Jeremiah 29:11-13, KJV

This is the sacred rhythm of life:

> We begin as **soil**, receive the **seed**, develop
> **roots, prune** what doesn't promote growth,
> and bear **fruit**.

We are formed in hidden places so that, in
time, we may reveal the handiwork of the Creator.
Every storm, every drought, and every season of
stillness has purpose. *I See Men As Trees* is not simply
a reflection on nature—it is a revelation of the divine
pattern within us all.

Just as the garden depends on seasons, so,
too, does the soul. Our lives unfold through the same
holy order: what is buried is still alive, what is hidden
is not lost, and what is tended in faith will, in time,
flourish.

Let this book remind you that growth is sacred work—that becoming is not a single act, but a lifelong journey. You are soil that can be renewed, a seed that can be awakened, roots that can go deeper, and a life that can bear fruit that remains.

As each chapter unfolds, you'll be invited to share in my family's journey through heartfelt stories and personal text messages. You'll find moments inspired by nature to help you feel connected, reflections to remind you of essential truths, and gentle calls to action designed to inspire, encourage, and center you on your own path.

It is my most profound honor to join you on this journey of soul work!

-ORANGES FROM MAINE-

He spoke of trees, from the cedar tree that is in
Lebanon, even unto the hyssop that springeth out of
the wall.

—1 Kings 4:33, KJV

The Gospel according to Mark describes a
conversation between Jesus and a blind man. Jesus
and his twelve disciples were traveling to Bethsaida
when a blind man was brought to Him. The crowd
begged Jesus to touch the man. Jesus took the man
by the hand and led him out of the village. There,
away from the crowd, doubters, and naysayers, a
remarkable conversation occurred.

After spitting on the man's eyes and laying
hands on him, Jesus asked, "What do you see?" The

man's initial answer was, "I see men walking as trees." It is this conversation with Jesus and the life of my mother that inspires the elements of this book. Trees are often used as a symbol for humanity in childhood fables, myths, poems, and Holy Scripture. My mother's loving touch on the eyes of my soul shines through me, bringing out my humanity, and I am all the better for it.

I have often heard, "Bloom where you are planted." Essentially, this means you should be fruitful no matter where you are planted. After deep conversations with my friend, Joel Buys, about trees, my perspective on this topic has changed. I explored the top-rated internet search engine and couldn't find a single vendor selling oranges grown in a grove across Maine. Blooming where you are planted doesn't happen without significant effort to create the right conditions; even then, many factors matter. Chances are, you've never seen an orange grow from a grove in Maine because the conditions aren't ideal for that tree to bear fruit there. The seed may be sound, the roots might dig deep, but if the climate resists its nature, the tree struggles. The same is true for us.

The phrase, "Bloom where you are planted," can be misleading because it shifts all responsibility for growth onto the individual, as though divine design, environment, and cultivation play no part. Growth requires partnership—between the soil and the seed, the gardener and the garden. Leaders must be discerning and work to create the right conditions for growth. The tools, timing, and tenderness of leadership determine whether a grove thrives or languishes. The wise leader learns to test the soil, to prune, when necessary, and to shelter young shoots from harsh winds until they can withstand the elements on their own.

This by no means removes responsibility from the individual [tree]. Every person must still reach for light, still drink deeply from the water provided, and still stretch roots into the unseen depths of faith and discipline. If you are leading in any capacity, look around at the trees in your family, community, or organization … are they dead,

suffering, coping, or fruitful?

June 2, 2021 @ 8:28 pm CST

> Hey Aunty and Uncle Team,
> Mom has been diagnosed with pancreatic cancer (ductal adenocarcinoma), which is the most common form. This message is intended to ensure we keep y'all in the loop as we all start this journey with Mom.
> The mass is in the body of the pancreas. Because of the biopsy she had done while in the hospital, she was diagnosed as stage 3. However, the doctors noticed two abnormal masses in her lungs and have ordered an additional biopsy to be done on those as well. If those cells in the lung are cancerous, then she will be diagnosed with stage 4 pancreatic cancer (because the cancer has started to spread). She has chosen to go to a treatment center with a multidisciplinary and holistic approach. The plan is to do chemotherapy for a few months and then shift to radiation (if it is stage 3) and chemotherapy (if it's stage 4).

The Model from Nature:

There was a winter when the orange grove nearly died. The cold came early that year—sharp, unrelenting, and without warning. The farmer and his family worked through the night, burning small fires between the rows to save what they could; their breath rose like smoke in the frozen dawn, and their bodies shivered for warmth as the wind blew. When the sun's rays finally climbed over the horizon, they revealed branches heavy with frost and fruit that had turned to stone in the cold. Many trees stood silent, brittle, appearing lifeless and defeated as the sun broke the crest of dawn.

But what the frost touched, it could not destroy. Beneath the hardened bark, life remained. The stubborn roots still remembered the warmth of summer, their purpose, and the change of seasons. The trees that looked most wounded held a stoic strength, sending their energy downward to preserve the core. When spring returned, new shoots emerged—small, persistent, vibrant green against the circumstance of frost. The next harvest came later than usual, but the oranges were richer, their sweetness deepened by the struggle. The frost had changed each tree—not by making them weaker, but by teaching them endurance.

That grove became a story among the growers: the trees that had endured the freeze produced the sweetest fruit. So, it is with us. Sometimes, the seasons that seem to steal our vitality are the very ones that refine our strength and help us survive. The cold may strip us, but it cannot reach what is rooted deep in faith. What once felt like loss becomes the slow making of sweetness—fruit that feeds others with the sweetness of perseverance.

Chapter Reflection: The Climate of Growth

This is the lesson of leadership, and the law of life: ***you cannot demand fruit from a place you have not tended.***

Every environment we inhabit—families, teams, congregations, and communities—has a climate. And whether we realize it or not, we are all climate-makers and barometers. Our words, our tone, our patience or impatience, and our grace or lack of it—all of it sets the temperature for growth.

The orange cannot change the weather, but the gardener can build shelter, redirect water, or nourish the soil to sustain life. The wise leader knows when to create warmth and when to provide shade, when to prune and when to rest. Perhaps the question isn't simply, *"Are you blooming where you are planted?"* but rather, *"What kind of atmosphere are you cultivating where you are?"* Because soil remembers how it has been treated, roots respond to care—fruit answers to faithfulness.

Call to Action and Reflection:

1. Examine your grove.

Look honestly at the spaces where you lead or belong. What kind of climate exists there? Is it one of fear, fatigue, or flourishing? Write about the spiritual temperature you sense around you and what it reveals about your leadership or influence.

_____

_____

_____

_____

_____

_____

_____

_____

_____

_____

_____

_____

_____

_____

2. Partner with the elements.

What external forces shape your environment—
culture, workload, and seasons of transition? How
might God be inviting you to work *with* those
conditions rather than against them, trusting that His
design still holds purpose in each season?

_____

_____

_____

_____

_____

_____

_____

_____

_____

_____

_____

_____

_____

_____

3. Tend the dry ground.

Where have you withheld nourishment—
encouragement, attention, and compassion from
those under your care? Reflect on what "irrigation"
looks like in your context. Who or what needs a
steady flow of life from you today?

_____

_____

_____

_____

_____

_____

_____

_____

_____

_____

_____

_____

_____

_____

-SOIL-

We are pressed on all sides, but not crushed;
perplexed, but not in despair; persecuted, but not
abandoned; struck down, but not destroyed.
—2 Corinthians 4:8-9, NIV

We must choose to be fertile ground. But at this particular stage of life, my stomach twisted in knots ... this was the great unknown. I had never felt fear like this, and nothing could have prepared me for this moment. My breathing was shallow; I noticed it and consciously tried to take deeper breaths. Nevertheless, regardless of how much oxygen I attempted to pull into my empty lungs, there wasn't enough—not enough room, not enough days, not enough prayer, and not enough tears to keep me from this intense moment of panic. I am living proof of surviving life with a broken heart, not because I wasn't prepared for this moment, but because I didn't like how my love had to leave this world.

I take pride in being able to change my destiny through sheer determination, discipline, and willpower. The softness of my mother's voice echoed in the chambers of my heart: "Be on the journey with me." However, for the first time in my life, it felt like things were happening to me, rather than me making things happen.

Early on a Tuesday morning, at the conclusion of a staff meeting, I was in deep conversation with a colleague when the vibration of my silent phone snatched me back to reality, startling me. As I retrieved it from my cargo pocket, the picture of my little sister smiling in earmuffs, gloves, and a hat, which usually brought me joy, overwhelmed me with sadness. I looked back up in slow motion and with heaviness in my voice, said, "I have to take this; my sister is calling to let me know my mother has passed away."

As I walked to the foyer of the building and sat on the couch, I answered the call. In a frenzied panic, and I could tell she was overwhelmed with tears, Domonique told me that she had just received a call that our mother had died. She had just left the house to run some errands and was turning around to make her way back to see for herself, make sure, fix it, stop this moment from happening, pray ... do something.

I looked up to see multiple people from the staff meeting standing in the hallway looking toward me. My commander, Mike Olson, walked over and asked me if everything was okay. He was informed that my colleague believed he had heard me say I had to take a call because my mother had just passed away. For the first time in two years, after many drives back and forth to Chicago, after late-night calls to let him know that I needed to take leave to fly home the following morning, I was now telling him I was not okay.

I left work and drove home. Once I arrived [still on the phone with Domonique], I was greeted by my wife. Her words caused the reality of the moment to sink in further. "What's wrong with you? You never come back home this early." My response was short and stoic: "Mom has transitioned to eternal life."

The entirety of my existence had come to a screeching halt, but the world was spinning, and people moved all around me. My empty screams fell lifelessly on the beach in the sands of time.

In every moment, I am the culmination of many things: prayers of my ancestors, love of my family, and fruit of my mother's branch. I am sure that the purpose of living is found along the journey of seeking. It is there on the path that we will find our treasure.

"Demetrius Nathan Booth," I own this name; in fact, I inherited it. It belonged to my great-grandfather, my grandfather, my uncles, and my aunts. More importantly, my mother gave me this name. That makes it mine. As far back as I can remember, my Aunty Team has always said,

"Nephew, your name will get there long before you do. Carry our family name with pride."

Recently, I discovered that they had claimed this wisdom from their mother, Annie Booth. A name is more than just letters strung together with thoughts or syllables perched on our lips; more intuitive than vibrations of vocal cords; it's the embodiment of the soul. My beginnings were forged in darkness and crowned with glory. Spoken into life and allowing my existence to manifest, it was a declaration to the universe that I exist. Just as God spoke at the heralding of existence, and it was so, my mother gave life to me in this world by calling me her son. A seed planted isn't dead; it is in the place of struggling, striving, and strength.

The darkness of the wilderness is never meant to break you; the darkness was designed for you to break into yourself. The wilderness prepares you for the calling to come.

One year, with tears in her eyes and a swelling of pride in her voice, my mother recorded a birthday message for me. In the most beautiful key, she sang "Happy Birthday" to her oldest child. There was a pause that caught me off guard. She told the story of my birth from the most loving perspective, having long forgotten the pain of labor, the community shame of being a single black mother, raising me (I have always been strong-willed), and the daunting task of preparing me for a world that did not yet exist.

The discovery that she had a son happened the moment the nurse placed me in her bosom. She recalled looking at my little face, my little lips, and my little eyes. The nurse asked her what she would name me, and her response was Demetrius Nathan Booth. It was at that moment she spoke into my life by proclaiming that I would be a man after her father's heart and that my life would honor him. My grandfather was my mother's hero.

June 4, 2021 @ 8:18 pm CST

Hey Aunty and Uncle Team, below is the latest update:
- June 4
Mom had a Positron Emission Tomography (PET) scan done today. The results will be back at some point next week. No specific date given. This test was done to identify if any cancer cells had spread to other parts of the body.
- June 14
She is scheduled for a biopsy of the nodules that were discovered in her lungs during the initial CAT scan that was done when they found the mass in the pancreas. Also, that same day she will get the chemo port placed in her chest.
Note: Quianna spoke with the social worker and she sent her information about support groups and disability benefits. Once we know what Mom's schedule will be for appointments to see her doctor and chemotherapy, I will pass it along to y'all in the event you want to take her to an appointment or support in other ways.

The Model from Nature:

In the quiet rows across vast stretches of farmland, soil carries both history and promise. It is not lifeless dirt—it is living earth, layered with stories of what once was and what can be. Every palmful contains particles of rock stripped down by time, organic matter from decayed plant life, and countless unseen organisms working tirelessly to recycle life into life again. Soil is more than a cylinder that cradles the seed; it shapes its future. Rich, fertile soil, cared for properly, breathes possibility into even the smallest seed. Yet, dry, depleted soil, left uncared for, resists growth, no matter how strong the seed's potential. Farmers and gardeners understand this truth: what you plant matters, but where you plant is equally important.

Healthy soil harmonizes holding and releasing. It holds water long enough for roots to drink and releases any excess. It stores nutrients, passing them on at the right moment, and it separates what is no longer useful, transforming decay into nourishment. Soil is patient, always preparing for seasons ahead, even as it sustains life in the present. But soil also remembers neglect.

When overworked without rest, it becomes exhausted and unable to give its best. When compacted, it hardens, keeping out water, air, and roots. When left untended, it invites weeds that choke and compete. The farmer who cares for the land must amend, replenish, and allow it to rest, for only then can it give again. From the garden and the field, soil offers its lesson: the unseen ground of life must be cultivated with care. The health of what grows above will always reflect the condition of what lies beneath. Soil whispers that what is sown in patience, tended with wisdom, and nourished with diligence will, in time, yield abundance.

Chapter Reflection: Preparing Your Soil

Beneath every mighty tree lies its soil—the unseen, quiet, life-giving foundation. Just as a tree cannot thrive on barren ground, you cannot flourish apart from the nourishment and support your life provides to your roots. Scripture reminds us, *"But blessed is the one who trusts in the Lord, whose confidence is in him. They will be like a tree planted by the water, that sends out its roots by the stream"* (Jeremiah 17:7-8, NIV). Your soil is not only the ground beneath you, but also your environment, your experiences, and the people and practices that feed your deepest self—your heart.

Take a moment. Examine your soil. Are your roots anchored in fertile ground, rich with truth, love, and purpose? Or is your soil rocky, thin, or crowded with distractions that stunt your growth? Just as a gardener tends the earth—removing weeds, enriching it with compost, and ensuring water reaches its depths—you, too, must intentionally prepare your life's foundation.

Consider the nutrients you need. Trees draw minerals, water, and organic matter from the soil to sustain leaves, branches, and fruit. Likewise, you must seek wisdom, courage, faith, and love to nourish your growth. Ask yourself:

1. *Which nutrients are missing in my life?*

2. *Where can I find what my soul needs to thrive?*

Reflect on how these elements will reach the deepest parts of your being, feeding your roots even when the storms of life blow strong. Look deeper still. Beneath the soil, trees connect through intricate networks of fungi and roots, sharing strength and resources in ways unseen. Your life is no different. Consider the networks that sustain you: mentors, friends, family, and faith communities. Recognize the invisible web of connection around you, and commit to both drawing from it and giving back, so that life may flourish in every direction. Remember your past seasons.

Soil carries the memory of rain and drought, of decay and renewal. Likewise, your experiences also shape your foundation. Reflect on the seasons you have weathered. Which moments have enriched your soil, making you resilient? Which seasons have hardened it, leaving it unyielding or depleted? Trust that even your hardest seasons can become nourishment, transforming struggle into strength, grief into wisdom, and loss into new growth. Finally, commit. Growth demands preparation. What intentional actions will you take to cultivate fertile soil—emotionally, spiritually, and mentally? How will you deepen your roots, strengthen your trunk, and prepare your branches to bear fruit in due season? As Psalm 1:3, NLT says, *"They are like a tree planted by streams of water, which yields its fruit in season and whose leaf does not wither."*

Your soil is yours to tend. It is where your roots drink, where your foundation strengthens, and where life begins to rise toward purpose. Prepare it well. Guard it. Nourish it. And watch as your roots sink deeper, your branches stretch higher, and your life bears fruit that endures.

Call to Action and Reflection

1. Examine your soil.

Think about the soil where your roots are planted. Is it fertile, rocky, or overrun with thorns? Consider the environments, relationships, and habits that support or block your growth. What can you cultivate, improve, or remove to prepare your soil for deeper roots?

_____

_____

_____

_____

_____

_____

_____

_____

_____

_____

_____

_____

_____

2. Identify the nutrients you need.

Just as trees rely on minerals, organic matter, and water, your life requires nourishment: wisdom, love, faith, and experience. List the "nutrients" you are missing. How will you seek them, and how will you allow them to reach your deepest roots?

_____

_____

_____

_____

_____

_____

_____

_____

_____

_____

_____

_____

3. Commit to preparing your soil.

Growth is impossible without preparation. Consider your daily practices, choices, and mindsets. What intentional actions will you take to cultivate fertile soil—emotionally, spiritually, and mentally—so that your roots may deepen, and your branches may bear lasting fruit?

_____

_____

_____

_____

_____

_____

_____

_____

_____

_____

_____

_____

-SEED-

Some seed fell by the wayside, and the birds
devoured it; some fell upon stony places, and were
scorched by the sun; some fell among the thorns and
were choked. But others fell into good ground and
brought forth much fruit.
—Matthew 13: 4-8, NKJV

True love requires that we give and make
sacrifices because, without consequence, sacrifice is
meaningless. Prayer is the transition statement for
life. It spans all tenses: past tense, as it is backward-
looking in thanks; present tense, as it allows us to
enumerate our blessings; and future tense, as it grants
us the courage to move toward the promise of God
that awaits.

The impact we have on others indicates the life we have lived. I have always taken the time to observe the world. At this point in my life, my mother reminded me of my nature as I sat and watched her. I imagine now that I just wanted to take her all in. All the bad seemed irrelevant as I considered the whole of who she was. The soul never dies; its state of being is transformed into something else beyond our understanding.

My mother was never one for keeping secrets. I would tell her that she was a pail with a hole in it. She would smile and say, "Well."

As the pancreatic cancer diagnosis was confirmed, she decided to attempt chemotherapy to give her children more time. She never wanted to do chemotherapy; one of her primary concerns was that it would crack the crown of glory that was her hair. Cancer is a devastating process; the journey is arduous for the patient, and it is heartbreaking for loved ones. As the disease progressed and the chemotherapy was ineffective, she grew weaker. Moments of independence vanished as she needed help standing up, sitting down, and even going to the bathroom.

At the time, unbeknownst to my younger brother, Wesley, and me, our mom held the best secret. Our sister, Domonique, is one of the most loving people created. As the youngest of my mother's five children, she was on her way toward marital bliss. In every moment of her life, she tries to figure out how she can do something for others, and this time was no different.

This willingness to love others led to the best-kept secret that my mom never told. It was all planned out. Since Wesley and I did not have the opportunity to do a formal mother-and-son dance because we didn't have traditional weddings, we missed out on that special moment. Domonique planned to yield the floor for us to do it at hers. At the time of the secret pact, only God knew that my mother's body would not make it to the day of the wedding. The secret was revealed only after my mother's passing.

In a phone call to Domonique to check in on her, the details of the wedding came up. With a tremble in her voice and tears of anguish flowing, she told me what she and Mom had been up to. "Mom and I had a secret, but I'm sure she already told you," Dominique exclaimed. We both laughed as I said, "Yeah, she probably did, but what was she supposed to keep between y'all?"

Barely getting the words out due to the disappointment in the hand life dealt, Domonique replied, "She was gonna dance with y'all at the wedding."

It was at this moment that my mother's unintentional-intentionality shone through. Now, fighting back my tears, I proclaimed, "Man ... that woman was something else." She must have known and given Wesley and me tons of dances to ensure the plan came to fruition.

During my visits home to take care of my mother, she would move back and forth as my hands supported her weight while helping her stand or sit, getting in and out of the car, or going to the bathroom. I would ask, "Are you trying to dance with me?" and she would reply, "Umm hmm." Without knowing, I was complicit in her plan to gift me tons of dances. It was only later that Wesley revealed that he would play music during the chemotherapy sessions and the two of them would two-step.

My mother's gifts to her children were planted as seeds of love. Even in the moments when she was less than perfect, despite trauma and hurt, she found a way, even in her passing, to teach life's most important lesson. With unintentional-intentionality, love was sown because that's all that could be found in the soil of her soul, and we are the fruit of it.

November 24, 2021 @ 11:59 am CST

Hey Aunty & Uncle Team,

Yesterday, Domonique took Mom to see her primary doctor. He gave her Allopurinol to treat the gout symptoms. She is walking better today. Below are her vitals. We are still concerned with the weight loss. We are praying that the week off from chemotherapy will also help with her appetite.

Weight: 107
Bp: 122/80
Heart rate: 80
O2: 100
Temp: 98.0

Thanks always for your support, love & prayers

The Model from Nature:

In the quiet of the forest floor, a tiny seed rests beneath the fallen leaves, half-buried in the soft, dark soil. To the untrained eye, it is insignificant, a mere speck among countless others. Yet within its unassuming shell lies the blueprint of life: the roots that will anchor, the stem that will break through resistance, the leaves that will stretch for the sun, and the fruit that will feed the world. The seed waits. It does not rush, does not demand recognition, and does not push against its environment before it is ready. It senses the moisture in the soil, the warmth of the sun filtering through the canopy, and the rhythm of the seasons. When the moment is right, it responds—subtle, deliberate, and unstoppable.

Its roots grow purposefully into the earth, unseen but intentional, seeking nourishment, stability, and connection to its life-giving force. They twist around stones, reach toward water, and intertwine with other roots, creating a hidden network of support. Above the surface, the first shoot appears slowly, tender, and fragile. It sways with the wind, weathers the storm, and leans toward the light, yet remains steadfast as it rises toward its goal. Every inch of growth requires a balance of patience and perseverance.

The seed teaches that greatness begins in humility and smallness. Its potential is enormous, but only when it surrenders to the process, when it trusts the soil, clouds, sun, and all the unseen forces around it. The purpose of life is not instantaneous; it is deliberate, seasonal, and often quiet. The seed reminds us that what is hidden, nurtured, and protected will eventually manifest with fruitful results. The seed is more than a beginning. It is a lesson: to wait, to root deeply, to embrace the resistance of the storm, to lean toward the light, to grow steadily, and to trust that what is planted in the right soil will bear transformative fruit.

Chapter Reflection: The Seed Within

Every tree begins as a seed, small, hidden, and vulnerable. Yet within that fragile shell lies the blueprint of strength, life, and purpose. The seed is patient, waiting in silence for the right conditions, trusting in unseen forces to nurture it, to awaken it, and to draw it toward the light. In you, there are seeds, too: gifts, dreams, callings, and untapped potential waiting for their moment to rise.

Consider the soil that surrounds your seed. Is it fertile, rich with love, faith, and wisdom? Or is it hardened, distracted, or neglected?

The soil determines whether your seed will remain dormant or push forth toward life. Reflect on the spaces you inhabit, the habits you nurture, and the people you allow near you. Are they tending the soil of your heart, or are they leaving it barren? Water, sunlight, and care are not luxuries; they are necessities. Seeds do not awaken through intention alone; they require consistent nourishment. Seeds do not demand immediate results. Growth follows its own seasons, and patience is its companion. You may not yet see the stem pushing through the soil, the first leaf unfolding, or the promise of fruit.

Yet beneath the surface, life is stirring. Reflect on the areas of your life where quiet growth is taking place. Reflect on your patience, your trust, and your willingness to remain steadfast while unseen progress takes root. Envision the fruit. Every seed carries the promise of life that extends beyond itself. What will your seeds become if you tend to them faithfully? What will they give to your life, your family, your community, and your world?

The seed is humble, but it is mighty. It reminds us that greatness often begins in silence, smallness, and patience. Tend your seeds. Guard them. Nourish them. Trust in their unfolding. And watch as the invisible work beneath the surface transforms into a life that bears fruit—steady, abundant, and enduring.

Call to Action and Reflection

1. Identify your seeds.

Consider the seeds within you: ideas, talents, gifts, and dreams. Which of these have been planted but not yet nurtured? Which are ready to grow? Reflect on what you are carrying that has the potential to bear fruit.

_____

_____

_____

_____

_____

_____

_____

_____

_____

_____

_____

_____

_____

2. Examine your environment.

Seeds can only grow in fertile, well-nourished soil
that is free from obstruction. What environments,
habits, or influences are helping or hindering your
growth? How will you cultivate the conditions
necessary for your seeds to thrive?

_____

_____

_____

_____

_____

_____

_____

_____

_____

_____

_____

_____

_____

_____

3. Commit to nurturing.

Seeds do not grow overnight—they follow their own seasons. A seed requires water, sunlight, and care to sprout. Which areas of your life require patience, trust, and surrender to timing? How can you learn to wait while still actively nurturing growth? What daily practices, disciplines, or spiritual habits will you commit to that will nourish your inner seeds? How will you consistently provide what they need to grow strong?

_____

_____

_____

_____

_____

_____

_____

_____

_____

_____

4. Visualize the fruit.

Every seed holds the promise of life and impact. Imagine the fruit that could come from your efforts if your seeds are nurtured and given time. How will this fruit bless your life and the lives of others? What steps can you take today to begin that journey?

_____

_____

_____

_____

_____

_____

_____

_____

_____

_____

_____

_____

_____

_____

-ROOTS-

That ye, being rooted and grounded in love.
—Ephesians 3:17, KJV

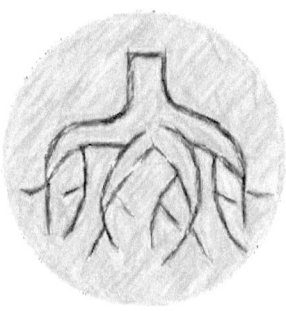

Every day you show up is a testament to the fact that you haven't given up. One of the most solemn moments I have experienced was helping my mother complete her paperwork after the initial oncology appointment and sitting next to her and my sister, Domonique, in the chair across from me, with our sister, Quianna, on Facetime. She was pregnant, and with the world still reeling from the effects of the global COVID-19 pandemic, it was decided that the best thing was for her not to come to the doctor's office and put herself and the babies at risk. When it was time to fill out the portion regarding the DNR wishes of my mother, I became overwhelmed with emotion.

A do-not-resuscitate (DNR) document is the most arduous act of love on a journey like this. It requires you to put the needs of your loved one above personal desire. I know it doesn't feel like it, but that's the surface of this moment. Yet, the negative voices of judgment in your head tell you this isn't love. It hurts, and you question yourself, your love, and your desire to protect them from life's worst, which enabled you to support their decision in the first place.

In moments and decisions like these, the best we can do is to keep showing up, prioritize being present, and caring for ourselves and others who are joining us on the journey. However, the first step to being courageous and holding on to hope is showing up!

I remember looking back at my mother and wondering what she was thinking and how this was impacting her. At the same time, I could not stop the floodgate of tears that poured forth. This was the first time I had to consider existence without my mom.

It's not lost on me that everyone dies; this happens to be the cycle of living in our fallen world. But for the first time, I was met with my mother's mortality in the form of a sheet of paper and her wishes not to be connected to tubes or experience the consequences of the process of having her body brought back to the medical terms of life. I could barely get the words out, in an attempt to comfort her, which, as I look back in hindsight, was more for me.

"I am going to be okay, it's just I love you so much, and this moment is overwhelming me, and I can't stop the tears. So, I will do the paperwork as I go through this." Then I asked if she was okay. I was only met with a head nod affirming she was. Domonique was already in tears, and seeing me hurting caused her to hurt more.

Research has surfaced indicating that if trees grow in an environment where they don't have to withstand wind resistance, their roots will not develop properly and will eventually succumb to the pressure of their weight. This process that trees go through is called building "stress wood." The lack of "stress wood," which is a critical element as trees grow, helps the tree become stronger. Without it, the trees can't thrive. The wind, acting as resistance, is vital for the tree to flourish and emerge as it was designed.

You may have heard that pressure makes diamonds. Similarly, without the resistance of obstacles and difficulties, we wouldn't develop properly. Don't complain about the trial; you are being tested, so God knows what's in your heart.

I am convinced that hope requires courage. Every day you stand, you are being strengthened. Every moment you don't quit, you are growing stronger. Each time you come back, your resolve deepens, and your roots spread deeper. I often think back to that moment; it felt as if the force of the wind was going to cause me to topple. All the while, I was developing "stress wood" that would allow me to stand amid the storm on the journey to come.

December 12, 2021 @ 6:05 pm CST

Hey Aunty/Uncle Team

Yesterday we got all my mom's grandkids together for our annual ThanksMas celebration. This was the first time we were all able to be present. She went home tired, but it was an awesome day.

The Model from Nature:

Down by the riverside, where the soil is dense and the earth meets flowing water, a network of roots stretches silently. They anchor trees against the pull of the current, weave through the sediment, and extend toward hidden pockets of moisture. Some dive deep, seeking the cool, steady reserves below; others spread wide, stabilizing the bank and supporting the life above. Each root, whether thick or fine, contributes to the strength, resilience, and vitality of the whole.

Roots in this place demonstrate patience and adaptability. They encounter rocks, shifting soil, and changing water levels, yet they continue to grow, probing, twisting, and adjusting to the environment. Their labor is unseen, but without it, the trees along the riverbank would topple, erode, or fail to flourish.

These roots also participate in quiet communication. Through the soil, they exchange nutrients, connect with fungi, and form a hidden network of mutual support with neighboring plants.

Life here depends on connection as much as on strength; no root grows in isolation.

Roots teach the power of hidden work. They labor in darkness, yet every struggle against stones, currents, and compacted earth strengthens them. They model resilience, humility, and persistence, reminding us that what rises above—the trunk, branches, leaves, and fruit—can only flourish when its foundation is deep, steady, and nourished. From the riverside, roots offer a living lesson: anchor deeply, adapt continually, connect meaningfully, and labor faithfully in the unseen. Strength is born in what lies beneath the surface.

Chapter Reflection: Rooted in Strength

Your roots are more than anchors; they are the unseen extensions of sustenance, resilience, and connection. They reach deep into the soil of your life, pulling in what nourishes your spirit, mind, and purpose. Take a moment to examine yourself:

1. Where do your roots reach?

2. Are they planted deeply in truth, faith, and unwavering values? Or are they shallow, vulnerable to the winds of circumstance and opinion?

Reflect on the sources that nourish you: experiences, mentors, and convictions. Consider the networks you are part of. Just as roots entwine with neighboring roots beneath the soil, forming connections that sustain and protect entire forests, so, too, must you nurture relationships that build, share, and multiply life.

3. Where are you connected?

4. Where do you need to extend your roots to find deeper nourishment?

Finally, commit to tending your roots with intention. Remove what chokes them, water what sustains them, and allow them to grow strong, deep, and unmovable.

Call to Action and Reflection:

1. Map your roots.

Trace the origins of your strength. What experiences, values, and relationships form the foundation of your life? Which roots have nourished you well, and which need attention or renewal?

_____

_____

_____

_____

_____

_____

_____

_____

_____

_____

_____

_____

_____

2. Examine your depth.

Consider the depth of your root system. Is it anchored in love, enduring truth, faith, and purpose, or weak and shallow, exposed to every storm? What steps will you take to deepen your roots?

_____

_____

_____

_____

_____

_____

_____

_____

_____

_____

_____

_____

_____

_____

_____

3. Identify what chokes your roots.

Just as roots can be crowded by rocks, weeds, or compacted soil, life can limit growth. What habits, fears, or influences are choking your roots? How will you remove or transform them to allow life to flow freely?

_____

_____

_____

_____

_____

_____

_____

_____

_____

_____

_____

_____

_____

_____

_____

4. Prepare for storms ahead.

Roots provide resilience during adversity, "stress wood." Reflect on the storms you have faced and the ones you may face. How will you nurture your roots so that you not only endure challenges, but grow stronger through them?

_____

_____

_____

_____

_____

_____

_____

_____

_____

_____

_____

_____

_____

_____

_____

-PRUNING-

Every branch in Me that does not bear fruit He takes
away; and every branch that bears fruit He prunes,
that it may bear more fruit.

—John 15:2, KJV

Three seasons had passed, along with several
holidays that held no meaning in the place we stood
in life. Not in the sense that I had been counting or
that the tasks performed wore on me in any
particular way. Mom had been undergoing
chemotherapy for six months now. Physically, her
body had been ravaged by the cocktail of
medications, and her spirit bludgeoned by
circumstance along the journey. Because I wasn't
physically collocated with my family in Chicago, I

didn't see the daily loss of weight or the toll the process was exacting. Once a month, as I traveled home to take her to treatment or spend time with her, I could see the visible effects of the journey.

As the new year approached, she decided to take a rest from chemo and recharge spiritually. This moment weighed differently on all her children; there were elements of staying the course and giving her as much time as possible under the belief that the chemo was slowing the growth of the cancers, and the other was ensuring she had more good days than anything else. "I am team good days and not team long days!" were the ill-spoken words that flowed from my heart. I had a conversation with my mother, and I knew she no longer wanted to endure the regimen of chemo. At the time, I didn't realize one had to be excluded from the other. We had no control over whether a day was good or if her life would be longer.

Her request from the onset was "be on the journey with me." The only thing we had a vote regarding was whether the days were good. As Mom heard us out, she spoke her final decision with confidence, "I don't want to go back to the doctor." At the time of the diagnosis, we had no idea that we would have exactly one year to spend with Mom here in this natural world. I'm not sure what we would have done or the decisions we would have made if we had known we had 365 days: one summer, one fall, one winter, one spring, 365 sunrises and sunsets, one more birthday celebration for her and her twin brother … one more Mother's Day.

As I reflect, I do so without regret. I don't regret trimming away things that didn't add value to life; I'm not bothered by the things I didn't do or the money spent to ensure we were present, the hours driven from Mississippi to Chicago, the last-minute flights to check on her, or the work we put in to keep our family hopeful, honor Mom's life, and say a heartfelt goodbye. We all stepped out on this unknown journey together.

May 21, 2022 @ 8:22 pm CST

Hey Aunty/Uncle Team:

Happy Mother's Day ... what would all us kids do without y'all, I'm glad we never have to find out. Y'all make this world and this family better. We stand on your elevated shoulders, love y'all. We just made it to the house, Mom sat in my chair and went right back to sleep, but I had her up early. She had a rough night yesterday, but we got it figured out, thanks to Aunty-Mama Scooby and those praying Wheaton kids to help me set her up and make sure she was comfortable.

Model from Nature:

"Pruning is mercy, not loss," her father would say every year during pruning season. "Each cut is intentional. Each removal is necessary." As a child, she didn't understand it. She only knew the routine; in the heart of the grove, pruning season always arrived with a silent stillness. There were no joyous songs of harvest or blossoms of spring—only the sound of shears and the slow fall of what once was alive. To the approaching untrained eye, at first glance, it may have looked like destruction, but to the grower, pruning was an act of mercy.

Now, years later, she sat motionless with a loss of words. They had spent all they had, prayed with fervency, and sought all the doctors and healers they could. The last voice was quiet but certain, "There is nothing more to be done. This is final, make your plans and prepare to say goodbye." What remained was a choice between longer days or gentler ones. More time or greater peace, fighting or resting. She retreated to the grove once more, and the branches that stretched too far, that would shade the fruit or steal the strength meant for growth, had been gently cut away. The cultivator knows that unchecked growth is not always good growth.

She knelt beside her favorite tree amongst the fallen branches, its leaves still green, and whispered a prayer. Not for more days, but for good ones, not that life was easier, but for strength. And grace enough to endure the cut. Rising to her feet, she was greeted by the sweetness of the trees exhaling as if they understood. As she looked back toward the house where the family sat together, she felt something shift inside of her. Her fingers ran along a freshly cut branch; the trees stood still, almost reverent to the moment.

A branch that grows wild bears leaves but not fruit. Pruning returns the tree to its purpose. If you walk through a grove just after the pruning, you'll see branches scattered on the ground—healthy, green, and full of potential. Yet, despite how alive they appear, they can no longer bring forth life. It is a somber and sobering sight, yet one the cultivator bears with hope, knowing that what was removed made room for what is to come. Pruning is not punishment; it is preparation.

In that moment, she saw it clearly: what seems like loss is, in truth, the precision of a promise. Pruning was not about taking life away. It was about making room for what is eternal to grow. Only a tree that endures the cut can bear fruit that lasts.

Chapter Reflection: The Mercy of the Cut

Pruning is the paradox of grace; the truth that God removes even what appears healthy to make room for what is holy. The branch that bears fruit is not spared from the cut; it is chosen for it. Divine pruning is not rejection; it is refinement. When God prunes, He is not punishing us for being fruitful. He is preparing us to carry more. The Father sees beyond what we've produced to what we are still capable of becoming.

What He purges is never random. He cuts only what hinders the flow of life, what draws energy from purpose, or what blocks the light of His glory from reaching us fully. Pruning often feels like loss because we are attached to what once gave us meaning: relationships, titles, habits, or identities that served us for a season. Yet every pruning carries resurrection potential. What is removed from our lives creates sacred space for new life to emerge. But we have to choose what will fill that void.

God's shears are steady and sure. They never slip. Every cut is a conversation—His way of asking, *"Do you trust Me with what you cannot yet see?"*

To the human soul, pruning may feel like subtraction, but in the kingdom, it is multiplication. The cut is the beginning of greater capacity. The wound becomes the womb of increase.

Call to Action and Reflection:

1. Recognize the gardener's hand.

Reflect on a time when God removed something or someone from your life and you didn't understand why at the time. Looking back now, what fruit came from that season of loss?

_____

_____

_____

_____

_____

_____

_____

_____

_____

_____

_____

_____

_____

_____

2. Have the courage to yield.

Pruning requires surrender. Consider the areas of your life that look "full" but may not be fruitful. What areas of your life do you struggle to release to God's shears? What would trust look like if you stopped resisting and yielded to God's unchanging and steady hand?

_____

_____

_____

_____

_____

_____

_____

_____

_____

_____

_____

_____

_____

3. Allow the cut to heal.

Healing after pruning takes time. What emotions or memories still ache from what was cut away? Write a prayer of gratitude for the way God is transforming the pain into purpose.

_____

_____

_____

_____

_____

_____

_____

_____

_____

_____

_____

_____

_____

_____

_____

4. Let the pruning feed others.

Every branch that remains becomes stronger, able to bear more fruit for others. How will your current pruning season prepare you to serve, mentor, or nourish those around you?

_____

_____

_____

_____

_____

_____

_____

_____

_____

_____

_____

_____

_____

_____

_____

_____

-FRUITFULNESS-

And he shall be like a tree planted by rivers of water, that brings forth his fruit in his season; his leaf also shall not wither; and whatsoever he does shall prosper.

—Psalm 1:3, KJV

Conflict is the crucible for character. "My heart is broken, and I am not sure I want that to change. I don't want this pain to hurt any less; I want to feel this, and I don't want this heartache to end. I will continue to live, but somehow the thought of enjoying life without you doesn't seem fair at all." These words echoed from my soul, reverberating through my consciousness, on an introspective note I had written in the margins of a book I was given.

I define grief as the deepest expression of love that has been stored up for a specific person with nowhere to go. Nothing is found nor lost. I believe we subconsciously place things so we can come or call upon them when we need them most. It is a token left by us as a reminder of our strength and purpose.

We are set on a path to remember through our experiences. On purpose, with purpose, and for a purpose, I found myself in Chicago. There was this moment during a Duo video call with my mother, when I noticed she was not in high spirits. My question, "Should I come home?" was met with a head nod because she could not muster words. I spent those nights on the floor next to her bed. There were instances when she forgot I was there because I decided to sleep next to her. When she called for me, I startled her. During one of the days present with her, I noticed that she had started to drift in thought. I called her back to me and asked where she had been.

"Thinking about home," she said as she looked back at me with those hazel-colored eyes.

"What's waiting for you over there?" I asked.

"My daddy, Nathaniel Booth, my mother, Annie, Joe, Margaret, George, and Greg." She paused in thought, "Tony and Billy Ray, you don't know them yet, but you will when you get there." This list of souls included the parents and siblings who had preceded her to eternal life. "And Jesus, Jesus will be there. You know what I want when I get there?"

With my heart in my throat, I responded with, "No ma'am, what do you want?"

"For Him to say, 'Well done, my good and faithful servant.'"

"Nothing for my journey now." These words now carry a deeper meaning for me. The reason there was nothing for my mother to carry on the journey during the last year of her life is that the seeds she planted produced a bountiful harvest. She didn't need to bring anything for the journey because the people accompanying her had brought everything required from this point forward. "Just be on the journey with me." Everyone showed up in their own way.

I will capture some of the offerings presented by her children, but also know that her husband, sisters, brothers, daughters-in-law, sons-in-law, grandchildren, nephews, nieces, lifelong friends, church family, and pastor all brought gifts of love to help along the way. My mother had five children that sprang forth from her womb, and one that was grafted in. It is from this perspective that I offer light, love, and fruitfulness of my mother's harvest.

In the wake of my mother's passing, the youngest of us carried the heaviest weight. Domonique had worked a full-time job and spent most days taking care of Mom post-shift. Notably, she worked twelve-hour shifts at the hospital. Her elements of love took the form of **caregiving**, **comfort**, and **protection**. She delved deep into reflection, expressing her desire to be the caregiver for Mom, as we had seen her be for everyone else. With tears in her eyes, she thought back on the comfort she provided as Mom endured procedures, and the protector came out during times when Mom couldn't speak up for herself or express what pain she was experiencing.

Mom would often affirm with my sister, Charlotte, that she was a good mother. Those seeds sprang forth as she strived to offer her special gift. Charlotte used her motherly instinct to ensure **comfort** and **dignity** were never lost. As you can imagine, as an adult, not being able to hold your drink, stand by your own strength, or wipe yourself can be damaging. "I always made sure Mom never lost her dignity, even when she had an accident and was so apologetic as I wiped her. I would remind her that she was loved and that it was okay. So, she never felt shame," Charlotte said.

Quianna's offering of love during Mom's last year with us brought a harvest of **rest** *and* **joy**. "The rest came in the form of, I didn't want Mama to have to worry about anything. No stress about bills getting paid, working the schedule for doctors' appointments, paperwork, and applying for Social

Security and disability. We all know I understood the assignment and gave Mom twins. My gift of joy came from Cailey and Caicey," Quianna shared.

My mother was number eight of sixteen children and happened to be a twin at that. We would all argue about who was Mom's favorite. I believe this was the thing that blessed her soul the second most. Once her grandchildren arrived, there was no question that they were all her favorites.

My brother, Wesley, was confident in his purpose on the journey, and so was everyone else. As I gathered the individual stories, everyone commented that they believed Wesley would say laughter was his purpose. He was the in-house comic relief growing up. There is no situation that he is going to take too seriously. I always hear him say, "Life is too serious all the time; we need to laugh." With an overwhelming sense of love, he proclaimed he brought *laughter*, *trust*, and a *listening ear*. "Laughter has always been my position, and how I loved her. Trust in the sense that she respected the man I have become, and that means the world to me, that she entrusted her health to me and honored my service to her," Wesley said.

In a moment of reflection, Wesley proclaimed, "My purpose is to be a nurse and take care of people. Based on my experience and expertise, she would come to me, tell me what the doctor said, and discuss it with me. I gave her a listening ear: When I took her to chemotherapy, I would ask about my father and manhood. She would tell stories so fluid and real, offering me a perspective not just of who he was, but of whom she became. Through all the tears, pain, and hurt, she deserved to laugh to help her forget cancer, even for a moment. Even as she was dying, she poured more love into us."

Cory is the son who was grafted in. Among us, we joke that I am Mom's firstborn, but Cory is the oldest child. In the wake of his father-in-law's transition to eternal life and the support he learned to give to his wife, Demeika, he purposefully brought intentional moments to deposit an environment of love along the journey. If you asked him, he would consider his contributions as small tokens to offset our collective efforts. The truth is, he surrounded her with positivity, making life all the richer.

Demeika has this instinct to love. "Sometimes you don't know what you need" is the proclamation she makes, with the love language written on her heart, informing the recipient that they are in a showering of care. With her blessing and sometimes instructions, Cory would fly into town every third month to take Mom to chemotherapy. One time, he brought her a beautiful basket of healthy snack options that we all credit Demeika for (he still claims he did it on his own … no one believes that). My mother never ate any of that healthy stuff. She preferred Pepsi, but she would show that basket to everyone. Good love will do that to you. It will put a pep in your step, a smile on your face, and hope in your heart. The token he brought was hope, and hope does not disappoint!

My offering on the journey was a **_reminder to look up_** and **_connections to love_**. During her visit to see me while I was stationed at Columbus Air

Force Base, my mother had a tough moment. I helped her to the bathroom, and I am not sure what it was that caused the fracture, but she cried out in anger to God. "I asked you to heal me and to help me." After she yelled it the third time, I responded with "Look up." As she looked up at me, I reminded her that "while the answer to healing may have been no, God sent you tons of help. If you are ever in question about that, all you need to do is look up, and you will draw strength because you are going to see me, Cory, Wesley, Quianna, Charlotte, and Domonique. If you ever feel down, all you need to do is …" and her response was simply, "Look up!"

It was time for me to take my mother back home. I had played the long game and coordinated ahead of time for her to be with me. Unknown to my siblings, it happened to fall during Mother's Day. My mother thought that was the funniest thing, that none of them paid attention to the dates that she would be with me.

As I knelt putting on her right shoe, she tapped both sides of my shoulders with her hands and said, "Y'all really did love me." Dismissive at first, I responded, "Yeah, chick, we love you … you loved us first. We still owe you some love."

Continuing my task of getting her ready, as I placed the left shoe on her foot, she tapped my shoulders again with both her hands and, in the most loving voice, repeated, "Y'all really did love me!"

This time, I paid attention, looking at her in those green-colored eyes, I reverted to the eleven-year-old kid who just wanted her to be okay. "Yes ma'am, we love you, we always have. You loved us first, and it's impossible not to give some of that back."

She smiled and responded with "Umm hmm, I know." Those were some of the last words my mother said to me before she transitioned.

We continue the journey to discover the other treasures she left behind. My mother needed nothing for her journey because the fruit of the seeds she planted brought forth caregiving, comfort, protection, dignity, rest, joy, laughter, trust, a

listening ear, hope, a reminder to look up, and a
connection to love.

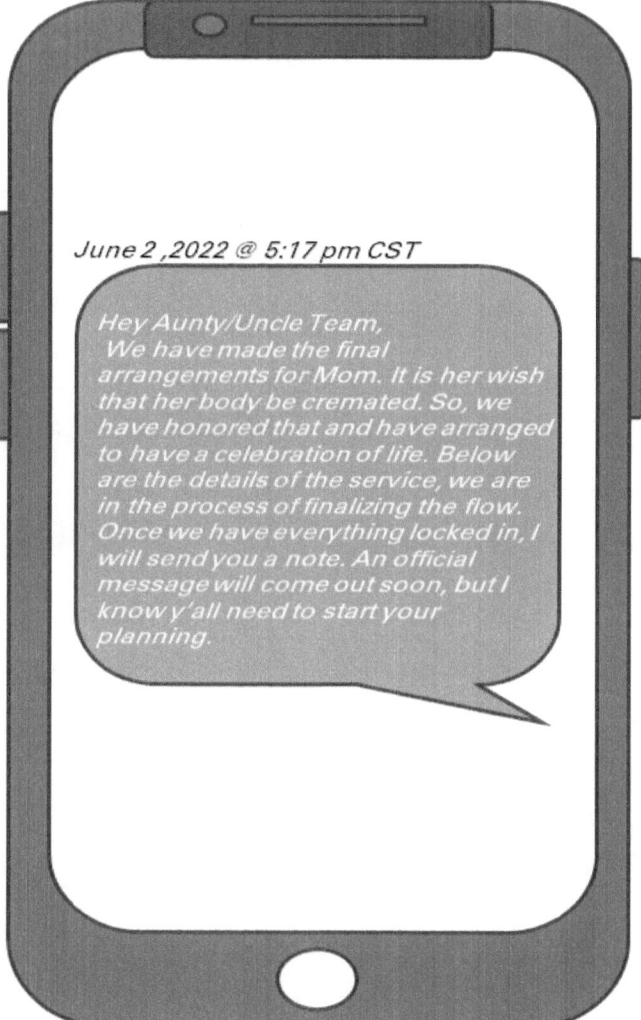

The Model from Nature:

I have experienced the sweetness of spring,
the sweltering heat of summer, the sharing of
harvest, and the stillness of winter. I have felt the
ache of pruning, the weight of wind, and the cold
indifference of winter. But now, the air is warm
again, and as I pull nourishment from the
environment, I feel life rising from the roots. It hums
through me like a hymn too ancient for words. It
reminds me of the purpose I was called forth to
bring and bear witness to.

I remember the pain of what was cut away,
yet I persist and stretch still toward light. And now, I
carry fruit—round, full, sweet, and fragrant. It is not
my doing; I only received what the Gardener sent.
Children come and reach for what I bear. Their
laughter shakes my limbs, their joy warms my roots,
and I feel their small hands steady against the
strength of my bark as they pluck the sweetness I
once held close. They cannot understand that this
moment began long before their existence, that I
held this day of promise inside of me, and I

withstood the process. I have seen many things in my life and have experienced centuries of human existence. I have learned that giving is to live.

I am not afraid of the weight. The fruit bends me low, but even in my bowing, I find purpose. The Gardener walks through the grove at dawn in the coolness of the day, tracing His fingers along my branches, whispering thanks. And I know I am seen. Fruitfulness is not a reward; it is a relationship. It is what happens when roots stay hidden, branches remain open, and the Gardener's hand is trusted through every change of season. Through all things, I endure.

And because I remain, I overflow.

Chapter Reflection: Known by Our Fruit

Fruitfulness is not a single event; it is a rhythm. It follows the long obedience of seasons— cultivating, sowing, tending, rooting, pruning, waiting, and harvest. The fruit we bear is not proof of our strength, but of our surrender. In Scripture, fruit always points beyond itself. The vine does not exist for its own abundance but for nourishment, witness, and continuity. *"By this My Father is glorified, that you bear much fruit; and so prove to be My disciples"* (John 15:8, NKJV).

True fruitfulness is the visible evidence of invisible trust. It emerges where patience meets pruning, where hidden obedience becomes visible grace. The fruit-bearing life is costly. The branch that bears much must carry weight. To be fruitful is to be willing to give away what God grew through you— your wisdom, your compassion, and your story. You are not the keeper of the fruit; you are the steward of it! The fruitful tree does not compete with others in the grove. It does not measure its branches against the next. It simply yields what it was made to generate. Each tree glorifies the Gardener in its own appointed season.

If you find yourself in a season of abundance, give freely. If you are still waiting for fruit to form, remain faithful. The Gardener wastes no season. He is working even amidst the darkness and the silence of the night.

Call to Action and Reflection:

1. Examine the weight you carry.

Fruitfulness bends the branch low. Reflect on where you feel stretched or burdened. Is it possible that what feels heavy is the evidence of what God has grown through you?

_____

_____

_____

_____

_____

_____

_____

_____

_____

_____

_____

_____

_____

2. Give freely from what you've grown.

Identify the "fruit" your last season produced—
wisdom, compassion, resilience, or testimony. Who is
reaching for it? How can you share it intentionally
this week?

_____

_____

_____

_____

_____

_____

_____

_____

_____

_____

_____

_____

_____

_____

_____

3. Stay rooted in the source.

Fruit without connection soon rots. Consider your spiritual rhythm: prayer, stillness, Scripture, and rest. Where is your connection thinning, and how can you deepen your dependence on the Vine?

_____

_____

_____

_____

_____

_____

_____

_____

_____

_____

_____

_____

_____

_____

_____

4. Celebrate Others' Fruit

Envy has no place in the grove. Reflect on how you can encourage and honor the fruitfulness of others. The grove flourishes when each tree gives thanks for the harvest beside it.

_____

_____

_____

_____

_____

_____

_____

_____

_____

_____

_____

_____

_____

_____

-LOVE IN AN UNEXPECTED PLACE-

Surely the LORD is in this place; and I knew it not.
—Genesis 28:16, KJV

I dedicate this chapter to the people who stopped for me. In Holy Scripture, God is expressed as the manifestation of love, *"the one who does not love does not know God, because God is Love"* (1 John 4:8, KJV). At any point you feel or experience it, it's because God is nearby.

In the wake of my mother's passing, I experienced some of the worst moments of my life. As the world continued to spin and life moved on for everyone, I noticed when people stopped for me. It came when I expected it the least. My dear friend, Niecee, would pray for me, and when the Spirit of

God led her, she would call or text to check in. I never expected dad jokes to lift my spirits; Tanner (T-Dog) Barber and Daniel (Slim) Seifert always stopped in to make sure I smiled every morning, and T-Dog gave me a gift that changed my life.

Donald Staats would come by to share stories about his father, ensuring I knew I was never traveling alone. Bradley Bell reminded me of my strength and the people who wanted to give back to me because I had cared for them. Michael Olson was one of the most genuine human beings I have ever met. He cared for me in a way I never expected, purposefully seeing me and opening his heart to suffer with me. My Aunty/Uncle team, cousins, Branch 21 (Cory, Connie, Camille, Ira Jr., Demeika, Rika, and John), you mean the world to me, and your kindness strengthened my soul. How fortunate to be held together by people who had nothing to gain … they loved because that's what was in their souls.

July 27, 2022 @ 2:35 pm CST

Good afternoon, Aunty/Uncle Team,

I wanted to take a moment to communicate with y'all again. push some information to you all.

We would like to invite you to an intimate family gathering to place Mom's ashes in their final resting place. It is our wish/request to manage the numbers and keep this as intimate as possible. We are asking that no invites be extended outside of your branches. Everything will flow in the same manner as when we honored Uncle George. We will have a virtual option available for the siblings who cannot be physically present. I know there was a lot of traveling last month (Mom's celebration of life and family reunion).

Purpose: Placement of Mom's ashes
Date: July 29, 2022
Time: 2:30 pm
Location: Abraham Lincoln National Century

Model from Nature:

She had not meant to stay. The traveler came from a far country where the winds were warm and the soil familiar. Her hands bore the memory and scent of tilled earth; she had known the rhythm of the seasons and the whispers that spoke to her soul, guiding her to cultivate, sow, tend, root, prune, and harvest. But after a long season of loss, she began walking—carrying nothing but a small pouch of seeds she couldn't suffer to leave behind.

For weeks, she crossed barren plains and jagged hills in search of something she could not name. Her journey ended not in triumph, but in exhaustion—at the edge of a valley where no kind words were spoken. The soil there was thin, stony, and hard to work. Yet something in her spirit—a small still voice said, *"Rest here awhile."* The villagers watched curiously as she knelt in their neglected fields. They warned her nothing could grow there, that the ground was tired and the rains unpredictable. Still, she pressed her fingers into the soil—gripping some of it in her palm and bringing it to her nose, she smiled. *"It only looks barren,"* she said softly, *"but even weary ground remembers rain."*

Day after day, she worked the earth—loosening what was compacted, removing stones, listening to the quiet sighs of soil long forgotten. She planted not her best seeds, but the ones she had nearly discarded—the ones that had cracked from the weight of travel. At first, nothing came. The people mocked, shaking their heads in disapproval. Yet she remained—willing, watering, waiting, whispering to the ground as if it could hear. And then, one morning, the valley shimmered with green. Small shoots rose through the earth. The air smelled of beginning again.

The villagers began to join her. They brought their own seeds—worn, mismatched, even broken—and together they learned the rhythm of tending. When the harvest came, it was unlike anything they had seen: fruit sweetened by struggle, roots deepened by discipline, branches strong enough to bear both shade and sustenance. One evening, as the grove stretched and swayed in a golden light, the traveler realized something sacred: she had come to heal the soil, but the soil had also healed her.

Love had grown in the most unlikely place—not from ease, but from tension. The ground, once cursed and rejected, became her refuge. The people who once pitied her became her family. The valley she meant to pass through became home. And as the seasons turned, she taught them what she had learned on the journey—that every patch of earth, no matter how broken, carries the memory of Eden. You only have to trust the seed, tend the soil, endure the pruning, and believe that fruit will come.

Chapter Reflection: The God Who Plants
in Desolate Places

Love rarely shows up where we expect it. We look for it in soft meadows and quiet fields, but God often reveals His love among the cracks—between the disappointments, the failures, and the forgotten corners of our lives. Scripture is filled with stories of love in unexpected places: Moses found it in the desert, Ruth in a foreign field, Joseph in a prison cell, and the thief beside Jesus on the cross. King David recounts, *"Thou preparest a table for me in the midst of my enemies; Thou anoints my head with oil; My cup overflows ..."* (Psalms 23, KJV). Love is not bound by condition; it is defined through presence. It does not wait for perfect soil—it cultivates it.

There are seasons when our surroundings seem too complex for growth, too barren for beauty. Yet, if we look again, we may notice a small sprout rising from that impossible place. That sprout is grace. That is love's quiet defiance. The Gardener is not afraid of rocky ground. In fact, He specializes in it. He plants us in unlikely places so that His glory—

not our comfort becomes the story. When love takes root in a harsh place, it changes everything around it. Stones soften. Cracks widen for light to enter. Others see what should not be possible and begin to hope again.

Love in an unexpected place is more than a testament. It says to the world: *Life can still grow here.*

Call to Action and Reflection:

1. Identify your stony places.

Reflect on the areas of your life that feel hard, confined, or unyielding. What part of your story feels too barren for growth? Invite God to show you what seed He has planted there.

_____

_____

_____

_____

_____

_____

_____

_____

_____

_____

_____

_____

_____

_____

_____

2. Notice where love has already shown up.

Think back on moments when love surprised you—
in loss, failure, or isolation. What did you learn about
God's nature through that experience?

_____

_____

_____

_____

_____

_____

_____

_____

_____

_____

_____

_____

_____

_____

_____

_____

_____

3. Let the cracks become conduits.

The fractures in the stone became channels for water and light. What pain or weakness in your life might now serve as a pathway for God's love to flow to others?

_____

_____

_____

_____

_____

_____

_____

_____

_____

_____

_____

_____

_____

_____

_____

4. Be the sprout for someone else.

Sometimes your presence in another's hard place is the very sign of love they need. Who might need to see life growing through your endurance right now?

_____

_____

_____

_____

_____

_____

_____

_____

_____

_____

_____

_____

_____

_____

_____

D's Life Lessons

1. Resilience is the precursor to strength. It doesn't come from a workshop, seminars, or an internet video. It comes from weathering life's storms, whether by walking, crawling, standing, or on one's knees. Resilience is always viewed on the other side.

2. Not everyone comes equipped with the Tensile-Strength to hold you together, lift you, or carry you through the worst parts of life's journey. Some people are there for a season, understand that, and when the season is over, let them move on.